50 Cooking for One: Delicious Solo Meals

By: Kelly Johnson

Table of Contents

- Garlic Butter Shrimp with Rice
- One-Pan Lemon Herb Chicken
- Creamy Tomato Basil Pasta
- Teriyaki Salmon Bowl
- Avocado Toast with Egg
- Spicy Peanut Noodles
- Caprese Grilled Cheese
- Miso Soup with Tofu and Seaweed
- Beef and Broccoli Stir-Fry
- Stuffed Bell Peppers
- Egg Fried Rice
- Zucchini Noodles with Pesto
- Chili Lime Chicken Tacos
- Greek Chicken Salad
- Shepherd's Pie for One
- Cajun Shrimp and Grits
- Homemade Personal Pizza
- Breakfast Burrito
- Baked Mac and Cheese
- Coconut Curry Lentils
- Mug Omelet
- BBQ Chicken Wrap
- Teriyaki Tofu Stir-Fry
- Baked Sweet Potato with Black Beans
- Classic Caesar Salad with Grilled Chicken
- Shakshuka
- Spaghetti Carbonara
- Korean Beef Bulgogi Bowl
- Vegetable Fried Rice
- Sausage and Peppers Skillet
- Mango Chicken with Coconut Rice
- Tuna Salad Lettuce Wraps
- Crispy Chickpea and Avocado Salad
- Garlic Butter Steak Bites
- Honey Glazed Carrots with Chicken

- Simple Ramen Upgrade
- Quinoa and Roasted Veggie Bowl
- Pulled Pork Sliders
- Chicken Fajitas
- Stuffed Portobello Mushrooms
- Lemon Garlic Butter Cod
- One-Pan Sausage and Potatoes
- Spinach and Cheese Quesadilla
- Eggplant Parmesan
- Buffalo Chicken Wrap
- Shrimp and Avocado Salad
- Creamy Garlic Mushroom Chicken
- Lemon Dill Salmon with Asparagus
- Homemade Sushi Roll for One
- Peanut Butter Banana Oatmeal

Garlic Butter Shrimp with Rice

Ingredients:

- 1 lb shrimp, peeled and deveined
- 2 tbsp butter
- 1 tbsp olive oil
- 4 cloves garlic, minced
- 1/2 tsp paprika
- 1/2 tsp salt
- 1/4 tsp black pepper
- 1/4 tsp red pepper flakes (optional)
- 1 tbsp lemon juice
- 2 tbsp fresh parsley, chopped
- 2 cups cooked rice

Instructions:

1. Heat olive oil and 1 tbsp butter in a pan over medium heat.
2. Add garlic and sauté for 30 seconds.
3. Add shrimp, paprika, salt, black pepper, and red pepper flakes. Cook for 2-3 minutes per side.
4. Stir in remaining butter and lemon juice. Cook for 1 more minute.
5. Remove from heat and garnish with parsley.
6. Serve over cooked rice.

One-Pan Lemon Herb Chicken

Ingredients:

- 2 boneless, skinless chicken breasts
- 1 tbsp olive oil
- 1 tbsp butter
- 2 cloves garlic, minced
- 1 tsp dried oregano
- 1 tsp dried thyme
- 1/2 tsp salt
- 1/4 tsp black pepper
- 1 lemon, sliced
- 1/2 cup chicken broth

Instructions:

1. Heat olive oil and butter in a pan over medium heat.
2. Season chicken with oregano, thyme, salt, and pepper.
3. Sear chicken for 4-5 minutes per side.
4. Add garlic, lemon slices, and chicken broth. Cover and cook for 5-7 minutes.
5. Serve warm.

Creamy Tomato Basil Pasta

Ingredients:

- 8 oz pasta
- 1 tbsp olive oil
- 3 cloves garlic, minced
- 1 can (14 oz) crushed tomatoes
- 1/2 cup heavy cream
- 1/2 tsp salt
- 1/4 tsp black pepper
- 1/2 tsp red pepper flakes (optional)
- 1/2 cup fresh basil, chopped
- 1/4 cup Parmesan cheese, grated

Instructions:

1. Cook pasta according to package instructions.
2. Heat olive oil in a pan, add garlic, and sauté for 30 seconds.
3. Add crushed tomatoes, salt, pepper, and red pepper flakes. Simmer for 5 minutes.
4. Stir in heavy cream and basil, cooking for 2 more minutes.
5. Toss in cooked pasta and top with Parmesan.

Teriyaki Salmon Bowl

Ingredients:

- 2 salmon fillets
- 1/4 cup soy sauce
- 2 tbsp honey
- 1 tbsp rice vinegar
- 1 tsp sesame oil
- 2 cloves garlic, minced
- 1/2 tsp ginger, grated
- 1 cup cooked rice
- 1/2 cup steamed broccoli
- 1/2 avocado, sliced
- 1 tbsp sesame seeds

Instructions:

1. Mix soy sauce, honey, rice vinegar, sesame oil, garlic, and ginger.
2. Marinate salmon for 15 minutes.
3. Sear salmon in a pan for 3-4 minutes per side.
4. Serve over rice with broccoli and avocado. Sprinkle with sesame seeds.

Avocado Toast with Egg

Ingredients:

- 2 slices whole-grain bread
- 1 ripe avocado
- 1/2 tsp lemon juice
- 1/4 tsp salt
- 1/4 tsp black pepper
- 2 eggs (fried, poached, or boiled)
- 1/4 tsp red pepper flakes (optional)

Instructions:

1. Toast bread until golden.
2. Mash avocado with lemon juice, salt, and pepper.
3. Spread avocado on toast and top with eggs.
4. Sprinkle with red pepper flakes if desired.

Spicy Peanut Noodles

Ingredients:

- 8 oz noodles (rice or wheat)
- 2 tbsp peanut butter
- 1 tbsp soy sauce
- 1 tbsp sriracha
- 1 tsp sesame oil
- 1 tsp honey
- 1 clove garlic, minced
- 1/2 tsp ginger, grated
- 1/4 cup hot water
- 1/4 cup chopped peanuts
- 2 green onions, sliced

Instructions:

1. Cook noodles according to package instructions.
2. Whisk peanut butter, soy sauce, sriracha, sesame oil, honey, garlic, ginger, and hot water.
3. Toss cooked noodles in sauce.
4. Garnish with peanuts and green onions.

Caprese Grilled Cheese

Ingredients:

- 2 slices sourdough bread
- 2 tbsp butter
- 2 slices fresh mozzarella
- 2 slices tomato
- 3 fresh basil leaves
- 1 tsp balsamic glaze

Instructions:

1. Butter one side of each bread slice.
2. Layer mozzarella, tomato, and basil on the unbuttered side.
3. Drizzle balsamic glaze and close sandwich.
4. Grill over medium heat for 3-4 minutes per side.

Miso Soup with Tofu and Seaweed

Ingredients:

- 3 cups water
- 2 tbsp miso paste
- 1/2 cup cubed tofu
- 1/4 cup dried seaweed
- 2 green onions, sliced
- 1 tsp soy sauce

Instructions:

1. Heat water in a pot, but don't boil.
2. Stir in miso paste until dissolved.
3. Add tofu, seaweed, and soy sauce. Simmer for 5 minutes.
4. Garnish with green onions.

Beef and Broccoli Stir-Fry

Ingredients:

- 1/2 lb beef, thinly sliced
- 2 cups broccoli florets
- 2 tbsp soy sauce
- 1 tbsp oyster sauce
- 1 tsp cornstarch
- 1 tsp sesame oil
- 2 cloves garlic, minced
- 1/2 tsp ginger, grated
- 1 tbsp vegetable oil

Instructions:

1. Mix soy sauce, oyster sauce, and cornstarch. Toss beef in the mixture.
2. Heat oil in a pan, cook beef for 2-3 minutes. Remove.
3. Add garlic, ginger, and broccoli, stir-fry for 2 minutes.
4. Return beef to pan, toss, and cook for 1 more minute.

Stuffed Bell Peppers

Ingredients:

- 2 bell peppers, halved and deseeded
- 1/2 lb ground beef or turkey
- 1/2 cup cooked rice
- 1/2 cup diced tomatoes
- 1/4 cup shredded cheese
- 1/2 tsp salt
- 1/4 tsp black pepper
- 1/2 tsp Italian seasoning

Instructions:

1. Preheat oven to 375°F (190°C).
2. Cook beef, season with salt, pepper, and Italian seasoning.
3. Stir in rice and tomatoes.
4. Stuff bell peppers with the mixture.
5. Bake for 25 minutes, top with cheese, and bake 5 more minutes.

Egg Fried Rice

Ingredients:

- 2 cups cooked rice (cold)
- 2 eggs, beaten
- 1/2 cup mixed vegetables (peas, carrots, corn)
- 2 tbsp soy sauce
- 1 tsp sesame oil
- 1 clove garlic, minced
- 2 green onions, sliced

Instructions:

1. Heat oil in a pan, scramble eggs, then set aside.
2. Sauté garlic and vegetables for 2 minutes.
3. Add rice, soy sauce, and sesame oil, stir-fry for 3 minutes.
4. Mix in scrambled eggs and green onions.

Zucchini Noodles with Pesto

Ingredients:

- 2 zucchinis, spiralized
- 1/4 cup pesto
- 1 tbsp olive oil
- 1/4 cup cherry tomatoes, halved
- 1 tbsp Parmesan cheese

Instructions:

1. Heat olive oil in a pan, sauté zucchini noodles for 2 minutes.
2. Toss with pesto and cherry tomatoes.
3. Sprinkle with Parmesan before serving.

Chili Lime Chicken Tacos

Ingredients:

- 2 chicken breasts, diced
- 1 tbsp olive oil
- 1 tbsp lime juice
- 1 tsp chili powder
- 1/2 tsp cumin
- 1/2 tsp salt
- 4 small tortillas
- 1/2 cup shredded lettuce
- 1/4 cup diced tomatoes
- 1/4 cup sour cream

Instructions:

1. Toss chicken with olive oil, lime juice, chili powder, cumin, and salt.
2. Cook in a pan for 6-7 minutes until done.
3. Assemble tacos with chicken, lettuce, tomatoes, and sour cream.

Greek Chicken Salad

Ingredients:

- 1 cooked chicken breast, sliced
- 2 cups chopped romaine lettuce
- 1/4 cup cherry tomatoes, halved
- 1/4 cup cucumber, diced
- 2 tbsp feta cheese
- 2 tbsp Kalamata olives
- 1 tbsp olive oil
- 1 tbsp lemon juice
- 1/2 tsp oregano

Instructions:

1. Toss lettuce, tomatoes, cucumber, feta, and olives.
2. Add chicken on top.
3. Drizzle with olive oil, lemon juice, and oregano.

Shepherd's Pie for One

Ingredients:

- 1/2 cup ground beef or lamb
- 1/4 cup diced onion
- 1/4 cup mixed vegetables (peas, carrots, corn)
- 1/2 tsp Worcestershire sauce
- 1/2 cup mashed potatoes
- 1 tbsp butter
- 1/4 tsp salt
- 1/4 tsp black pepper

Instructions:

1. Preheat oven to 375°F (190°C).
2. Cook beef with onions, drain excess fat.
3. Stir in vegetables, Worcestershire sauce, salt, and pepper.
4. Transfer to a small baking dish, spread mashed potatoes on top.
5. Dot with butter and bake for 20 minutes.

Cajun Shrimp and Grits

Ingredients:

- 1/2 lb shrimp, peeled and deveined
- 1 tsp Cajun seasoning
- 1 tbsp butter
- 1 clove garlic, minced
- 1/2 cup grits
- 1 1/2 cups water
- 1/4 cup shredded cheddar cheese
- 1/4 tsp salt
- 1 green onion, sliced

Instructions:

1. Cook grits in water until thickened, stir in cheese and salt.
2. Season shrimp with Cajun seasoning.
3. Heat butter in a pan, cook shrimp with garlic for 2-3 minutes per side.
4. Serve shrimp over grits, garnish with green onions.

Homemade Personal Pizza

Ingredients:

- 1 small pizza crust or pita
- 2 tbsp pizza sauce
- 1/2 cup shredded mozzarella
- 6 pepperoni slices (or preferred toppings)
- 1/2 tsp Italian seasoning

Instructions:

1. Preheat oven to 400°F (200°C).
2. Spread sauce on crust, top with cheese and toppings.
3. Bake for 10-12 minutes.
4. Sprinkle with Italian seasoning and serve.

Breakfast Burrito

Ingredients:

- 1 large tortilla
- 2 eggs, scrambled
- 1/4 cup shredded cheese
- 1/4 cup cooked sausage or bacon
- 2 tbsp salsa
- 1/4 avocado, sliced

Instructions:

1. Lay tortilla flat, add scrambled eggs, cheese, meat, salsa, and avocado.
2. Fold sides in and roll into a burrito.
3. Serve warm.

Baked Mac and Cheese

Ingredients:

- 1 1/2 cups elbow macaroni
- 1 tbsp butter
- 1 tbsp flour
- 1 cup milk
- 1 1/2 cups shredded cheddar cheese
- 1/2 tsp salt
- 1/4 tsp black pepper
- 1/4 cup breadcrumbs

Instructions:

1. Preheat oven to 375°F (190°C).
2. Cook pasta, drain.
3. Melt butter, whisk in flour, and slowly add milk. Cook until thick.
4. Stir in cheese, salt, and pepper. Mix with pasta.
5. Transfer to a baking dish, top with breadcrumbs, and bake for 20 minutes.

Coconut Curry Lentils

Ingredients:

- 1/2 cup lentils
- 1 cup coconut milk
- 1/2 cup vegetable broth
- 1/2 tsp curry powder
- 1/4 tsp turmeric
- 1 clove garlic, minced
- 1/4 tsp salt

Instructions:

1. Rinse lentils and add to a pot with coconut milk and broth.
2. Stir in curry powder, turmeric, garlic, and salt.
3. Simmer for 20-25 minutes until tender.

Mug Omelet

Ingredients:

- 2 eggs
- 2 tbsp milk
- 2 tbsp shredded cheese
- 2 tbsp diced bell pepper
- 2 tbsp diced ham or cooked bacon
- Salt and pepper to taste

Instructions:

1. In a microwave-safe mug, whisk eggs and milk.
2. Stir in cheese, bell pepper, ham, salt, and pepper.
3. Microwave for 1-2 minutes, stirring halfway.

BBQ Chicken Wrap

Ingredients:

- 1 large tortilla
- 1/2 cup cooked shredded chicken
- 2 tbsp BBQ sauce
- 1/4 cup shredded cheese
- 1/4 cup shredded lettuce
- 2 tbsp diced tomatoes

Instructions:

1. Mix chicken with BBQ sauce.
2. Spread onto the tortilla, top with cheese, lettuce, and tomatoes.
3. Roll into a wrap and serve.

Teriyaki Tofu Stir-Fry

Ingredients:

- 1/2 block firm tofu, cubed
- 1 tbsp soy sauce
- 1 tbsp teriyaki sauce
- 1 tsp sesame oil
- 1/2 cup broccoli florets
- 1/4 cup bell peppers, sliced
- 1 clove garlic, minced

Instructions:

1. Toss tofu with soy sauce and let sit for 10 minutes.
2. Heat sesame oil in a pan, cook tofu until golden.
3. Add garlic, broccoli, and bell peppers, stir-fry for 3 minutes.
4. Stir in teriyaki sauce and serve.

Baked Sweet Potato with Black Beans

Ingredients:

- 1 medium sweet potato
- 1/2 cup black beans, drained
- 1/4 tsp cumin
- 1/4 tsp chili powder
- 2 tbsp sour cream
- 1 tbsp chopped cilantro

Instructions:

1. Preheat oven to 400°F (200°C).
2. Pierce sweet potato with a fork, bake for 45 minutes.
3. Heat black beans with cumin and chili powder.
4. Slice potato open, top with beans, sour cream, and cilantro.

Classic Caesar Salad with Grilled Chicken

Ingredients:

- 1 cooked chicken breast, sliced
- 2 cups romaine lettuce, chopped
- 1/4 cup croutons
- 2 tbsp grated Parmesan cheese
- 2 tbsp Caesar dressing

Instructions:

1. Toss lettuce with dressing.
2. Top with grilled chicken, croutons, and Parmesan.
3. Serve immediately.

Shakshuka

Ingredients:

- 2 tbsp olive oil
- 1 onion, diced
- 1 bell pepper, diced
- 2 cloves garlic, minced
- 1 tsp ground cumin
- 1 tsp ground paprika
- 1/2 tsp chili flakes
- 1 can (14 oz) crushed tomatoes
- Salt and pepper to taste
- 4 large eggs
- Fresh parsley, chopped

Instructions:

1. Heat olive oil in a pan, sauté onion and bell pepper until soft.
2. Add garlic, cumin, paprika, and chili flakes, cook for 1 minute.
3. Stir in crushed tomatoes, season with salt and pepper, simmer for 10 minutes.
4. Make wells in the sauce and crack eggs into them. Cover and cook until eggs are set.
5. Garnish with parsley and serve.

Spaghetti Carbonara

Ingredients:

- 8 oz spaghetti
- 2 eggs
- 1/2 cup grated Parmesan cheese
- 4 slices bacon, chopped
- 1 clove garlic, minced
- Salt and pepper to taste

Instructions:

1. Cook spaghetti according to package instructions.
2. In a bowl, whisk eggs and Parmesan. Set aside.
3. Cook bacon in a pan until crispy, then add garlic and cook for 1 minute.
4. Drain pasta, reserving some pasta water.
5. Toss pasta in the bacon mixture, then pour in egg and cheese mixture, stirring quickly to create a creamy sauce.
6. Adjust with pasta water for desired consistency. Season with salt and pepper.

Korean Beef Bulgogi Bowl

Ingredients:

- 1 lb ground beef
- 2 tbsp soy sauce
- 2 tbsp brown sugar
- 1 tbsp sesame oil
- 1 tbsp rice vinegar
- 2 cloves garlic, minced
- 1/2 tsp ginger, grated
- 1 green onion, sliced
- 1 cup cooked rice
- 1/2 cup sliced cucumber
- 1/4 cup kimchi (optional)

Instructions:

1. In a bowl, mix soy sauce, brown sugar, sesame oil, rice vinegar, garlic, and ginger.
2. Cook ground beef in a pan, then drain excess fat.
3. Stir in the marinade and cook for 2-3 minutes.
4. Serve beef over rice, garnished with green onions, cucumber, and kimchi.

Vegetable Fried Rice

Ingredients:

- 2 cups cooked rice (preferably cold)
- 1 tbsp sesame oil
- 1/2 cup mixed vegetables (peas, carrots, corn)
- 2 eggs, scrambled
- 2 tbsp soy sauce
- 1 clove garlic, minced
- 2 green onions, sliced

Instructions:

1. Heat sesame oil in a pan, add vegetables and cook for 2-3 minutes.
2. Push vegetables aside, scramble eggs in the same pan.
3. Add cooked rice, soy sauce, and garlic, stir-fry for 3-4 minutes.
4. Garnish with green onions.

Sausage and Peppers Skillet

Ingredients:

- 4 sausage links (Italian or your choice)
- 1 onion, sliced
- 2 bell peppers, sliced
- 1 tbsp olive oil
- Salt and pepper to taste
- 1/4 tsp red pepper flakes (optional)

Instructions:

1. Heat olive oil in a skillet, cook sausage links until browned, then remove and slice them.
2. In the same pan, sauté onions and bell peppers until soft.
3. Add sausage back to the pan, season with salt, pepper, and red pepper flakes.
4. Serve hot.

Mango Chicken with Coconut Rice

Ingredients:

- 2 chicken breasts
- 1 ripe mango, sliced
- 1 tbsp olive oil
- 1 tbsp lime juice
- 1/2 tsp chili powder
- 1 cup coconut milk
- 1 cup rice
- Salt to taste

Instructions:

1. Cook rice with coconut milk and a pinch of salt until tender.
2. Season chicken with lime juice, chili powder, salt, and olive oil. Cook in a pan until browned and cooked through.
3. Serve chicken with coconut rice, topped with fresh mango slices.

Tuna Salad Lettuce Wraps

Ingredients:

- 1 can tuna, drained
- 1/4 cup mayonnaise
- 1 tbsp Dijon mustard
- 1 tbsp pickle relish
- 1 tbsp fresh dill, chopped
- Salt and pepper to taste
- 4 large lettuce leaves (such as Romaine or Butter Lettuce)

Instructions:

1. In a bowl, mix tuna, mayonnaise, mustard, relish, dill, salt, and pepper.
2. Spoon mixture onto lettuce leaves and serve as wraps.

Crispy Chickpea and Avocado Salad

Ingredients:

- 1 can chickpeas, drained and rinsed
- 1 tbsp olive oil
- 1 tsp paprika
- Salt and pepper to taste
- 1 avocado, diced
- 2 cups mixed greens
- 1/4 cup red onion, sliced
- 2 tbsp olive oil (for dressing)
- 1 tbsp lemon juice

Instructions:

1. Toss chickpeas with olive oil, paprika, salt, and pepper. Roast at 400°F (200°C) for 25 minutes until crispy.
2. In a bowl, toss greens, avocado, and red onion.
3. Drizzle with olive oil and lemon juice, top with crispy chickpeas.

Garlic Butter Steak Bites

Ingredients:

- 1 lb sirloin steak, cut into cubes
- 3 tbsp butter
- 3 cloves garlic, minced
- Salt and pepper to taste
- 1 tbsp fresh parsley, chopped

Instructions:

1. Season steak cubes with salt and pepper.
2. Heat butter in a pan, cook steak bites for 3-4 minutes until browned.
3. Add garlic, cook for another 1 minute.
4. Garnish with parsley and serve.

Honey Glazed Carrots with Chicken

Ingredients:

- 2 chicken breasts
- 1 lb carrots, peeled and cut
- 2 tbsp honey
- 1 tbsp olive oil
- 1/2 tsp thyme
- Salt and pepper to taste

Instructions:

1. Cook chicken breasts in a pan until golden and cooked through.
2. In the same pan, add olive oil, honey, thyme, and carrots. Cook until carrots are tender and caramelized.
3. Serve chicken with honey-glazed carrots.

Simple Ramen Upgrade

Ingredients:

- 1 pack instant ramen
- 1 egg
- 1/2 cup spinach
- 1/4 cup sliced mushrooms
- 1 tbsp soy sauce
- 1 tsp sesame oil

Instructions:

1. Cook ramen noodles according to package instructions.
2. In the last minute of cooking, add spinach and mushrooms.
3. Crack an egg into the soup and stir to poach.
4. Add soy sauce and sesame oil for flavor, and serve.

Quinoa and Roasted Veggie Bowl

Ingredients:

- 1 cup quinoa
- 1 zucchini, chopped
- 1 bell pepper, chopped
- 1 cup cherry tomatoes, halved
- 1 tbsp olive oil
- 1 tsp garlic powder
- Salt and pepper to taste
- 1/4 cup feta cheese (optional)
- 2 tbsp tahini or dressing of choice

Instructions:

1. Preheat oven to 400°F (200°C).
2. Toss zucchini, bell pepper, and cherry tomatoes with olive oil, garlic powder, salt, and pepper. Roast for 20-25 minutes until tender.
3. Cook quinoa according to package instructions.
4. Serve quinoa in bowls, top with roasted veggies and feta. Drizzle with tahini or your favorite dressing.

Pulled Pork Sliders

Ingredients:

- 2 lbs pork shoulder
- 1/2 cup BBQ sauce
- 1/4 cup apple cider vinegar
- 1 tbsp brown sugar
- 1 tsp smoked paprika
- 1 tsp garlic powder
- 8 slider buns
- Coleslaw (optional)

Instructions:

1. Slow cook pork shoulder on low for 8 hours with BBQ sauce, apple cider vinegar, brown sugar, paprika, and garlic powder.
2. Shred pork using two forks.
3. Serve pulled pork on slider buns with coleslaw if desired.

Chicken Fajitas

Ingredients:

- 2 chicken breasts, sliced
- 1 bell pepper, sliced
- 1 onion, sliced
- 2 tbsp olive oil
- 1 tsp chili powder
- 1 tsp cumin
- 1/2 tsp paprika
- Salt and pepper to taste
- Flour tortillas
- Lime wedges

Instructions:

1. Heat olive oil in a pan, add chicken slices, and cook until browned.
2. Add bell pepper, onion, chili powder, cumin, paprika, salt, and pepper, and cook until vegetables are tender.
3. Serve chicken and veggies in tortillas with lime wedges.

Stuffed Portobello Mushrooms

Ingredients:

- 4 large Portobello mushrooms, stems removed
- 1/2 cup ricotta cheese
- 1/4 cup spinach, chopped
- 1/4 cup mozzarella cheese, shredded
- 1 tbsp olive oil
- 1 tsp garlic powder
- Salt and pepper to taste

Instructions:

1. Preheat oven to 375°F (190°C).
2. Mix ricotta cheese, spinach, mozzarella, garlic powder, salt, and pepper.
3. Stuff mushrooms with the ricotta mixture and drizzle with olive oil.
4. Bake for 20 minutes until mushrooms are tender.

Lemon Garlic Butter Cod

Ingredients:

- 4 cod fillets
- 3 tbsp butter, melted
- 2 cloves garlic, minced
- 1 tbsp lemon juice
- 1/2 tsp lemon zest
- Salt and pepper to taste
- Fresh parsley for garnish

Instructions:

1. Preheat oven to 400°F (200°C).
2. Mix butter, garlic, lemon juice, lemon zest, salt, and pepper.
3. Place cod fillets on a baking sheet and drizzle with lemon garlic butter.
4. Bake for 12-15 minutes until fish flakes easily. Garnish with parsley.

One-Pan Sausage and Potatoes

Ingredients:

- 4 sausage links (Italian or your choice)
- 4 medium potatoes, diced
- 1 tbsp olive oil
- 1 tsp dried rosemary
- Salt and pepper to taste

Instructions:

1. Preheat oven to 400°F (200°C).
2. Toss diced potatoes with olive oil, rosemary, salt, and pepper. Spread on a baking sheet.
3. Add sausage links to the pan and bake for 25-30 minutes until sausage is cooked through and potatoes are tender.
4. Serve hot.

Spinach and Cheese Quesadilla

Ingredients:

- 2 flour tortillas
- 1 cup fresh spinach, chopped
- 1/2 cup shredded mozzarella cheese
- 1/4 cup shredded cheddar cheese
- 1 tbsp olive oil
- Salt and pepper to taste

Instructions:

1. Heat olive oil in a pan over medium heat.
2. Place one tortilla in the pan and top with spinach, mozzarella, and cheddar.
3. Place the second tortilla on top, cook for 2-3 minutes, then flip and cook the other side until golden and the cheese is melted.
4. Slice and serve hot.

Eggplant Parmesan

Ingredients:

- 1 medium eggplant, sliced into rounds
- 1 cup breadcrumbs
- 1/2 cup grated Parmesan cheese
- 1 egg, beaten
- 1 cup marinara sauce
- 1 cup shredded mozzarella cheese
- 2 tbsp olive oil

Instructions:

1. Preheat oven to 375°F (190°C).
2. Dip eggplant slices into beaten egg, then coat with a mixture of breadcrumbs and Parmesan.
3. Heat olive oil in a pan and cook eggplant slices for 2-3 minutes per side until golden.
4. Place eggplant in a baking dish, top with marinara sauce and mozzarella.
5. Bake for 15-20 minutes until cheese is bubbly. Serve hot.

Buffalo Chicken Wrap

Ingredients:

- 1 chicken breast, cooked and shredded
- 2 tbsp buffalo sauce
- 1/4 cup ranch dressing
- 1 cup lettuce, chopped
- 1 tomato, diced
- 1 large flour tortilla

Instructions:

1. Toss shredded chicken with buffalo sauce.
2. Lay the tortilla flat and spread ranch dressing in the center.
3. Add chicken, lettuce, and tomato.
4. Roll up the tortilla to form a wrap and serve.

Shrimp and Avocado Salad

Ingredients:

- 1/2 lb cooked shrimp, peeled and deveined
- 1 avocado, diced
- 1 cup mixed greens
- 1/4 red onion, thinly sliced
- 1 tbsp olive oil
- 1 tbsp lemon juice
- Salt and pepper to taste

Instructions:

1. Toss shrimp, avocado, mixed greens, and red onion in a bowl.
2. Drizzle with olive oil and lemon juice, season with salt and pepper.
3. Serve immediately.

Creamy Garlic Mushroom Chicken

Ingredients:

- 2 chicken breasts
- 1 cup mushrooms, sliced
- 1/2 cup heavy cream
- 2 tbsp butter
- 2 cloves garlic, minced
- Salt and pepper to taste
- Fresh parsley for garnish

Instructions:

1. Cook chicken breasts in butter until browned on both sides. Remove and set aside.
2. In the same pan, sauté garlic and mushrooms until soft.
3. Add heavy cream, salt, and pepper, and simmer for 2-3 minutes.
4. Return chicken to the pan and cook for an additional 5-7 minutes, until the chicken is cooked through.
5. Garnish with fresh parsley and serve.

Lemon Dill Salmon with Asparagus

Ingredients:

- 2 salmon fillets
- 1 bunch asparagus, trimmed
- 1 lemon, sliced
- 2 tbsp olive oil
- 1 tbsp fresh dill, chopped
- Salt and pepper to taste

Instructions:

1. Preheat oven to 400°F (200°C).
2. Place salmon and asparagus on a baking sheet. Drizzle with olive oil and season with salt and pepper.
3. Place lemon slices on top of salmon and sprinkle with fresh dill.
4. Bake for 12-15 minutes until salmon is cooked through and flakes easily.
5. Serve hot with the roasted asparagus.

Homemade Sushi Roll for One

Ingredients:

- 1/2 cup sushi rice
- 1/2 cup water
- 1 tsp rice vinegar
- 1/2 tsp sugar
- 1/4 tsp salt
- 1 sheet nori (seaweed)
- 1/4 cucumber, julienned
- 1/4 avocado, sliced
- 2 oz cooked shrimp or crab meat (optional)

Instructions:

1. Cook sushi rice according to package instructions, then mix with rice vinegar, sugar, and salt.
2. Place nori sheet on a sushi mat, spread a thin layer of rice, leaving about an inch at the top.
3. Add cucumber, avocado, and shrimp (or crab) in a line across the rice.
4. Roll up the sushi tightly, using the mat.
5. Slice into bite-sized pieces and serve.

Peanut Butter Banana Oatmeal

Ingredients:

- 1/2 cup rolled oats
- 1 cup milk (or almond milk)
- 1 banana, sliced
- 1 tbsp peanut butter
- 1 tsp honey (optional)
- A pinch of cinnamon

Instructions:

1. Cook oats with milk according to package instructions.
2. Stir in peanut butter until melted and creamy.
3. Top with sliced banana, honey, and a sprinkle of cinnamon.
4. Serve warm.

www.ingramcontent.com/pod-product-compliance
Lightning Source LLC
LaVergne TN
LVHW081334060526
838201LV00055B/2633